ULTIMATE GRANDPARENT-GRANDCHILD EXPERIENCE COUPONS

A Keepsake Journal of

Grandparent–Grandchild Memories

Joy Holiday Family

We do not remember days, we remember moments.
Cesare Pavese

Copyright © 2021 by Joy Holiday Publishing
All rights reserved. No part of this book may be reproduced or used in any manner without written permission of the copyright owner except for the use of quotations in a book review.

Book Design by Joy Holiday Publishing LLC

978-1-956146-11-0

Images used under license from Canva.com

Capture the MOMENTS
while you make the MEMORIES

You're never too old to have fun! Grandparents and grandkids of all ages will treasure the memories they create using these experience coupons. Finger painting isn't just for toddlers! In this era of multigenerational homes and online video visits, it's the perfect time to be intentional about your family experiences. You know the grandparent/grandchild relationship is special, so get the perfect gift to stay connected. This book is the ultimate in coupon gift-giving. Fifty-two thoughtful and entertaining coupons for creating lifelong memories. Enough coupons to have one for each week of the entire calendar year.

This keepsake journal chronicles not just the gift giving, but also the actual redemption of the coupons. This gorgeous book takes the coupon idea to the next level. Each activity is designed as an elegant ticket. The large, easy-to-read coupon tickets and redemption stubs are intended to stay in the book. Next to each coupon page is a space to place a photo and write what you did together.

There is also an additional page of smaller coupons replicating the larger tickets that may be cut out as part of the fun. This book is the solution to unused coupon books or gifts that are not part of a larger experience. Families can look back on all the special experiences they created together throughout the year.

With these coupon prompts, grandparents get to spend quality time with their grandchildren doing the things they love or finding new ways to have fun! This book includes activities for families of all ages. We have even included some extra blank tickets since you know your family best. Are you a gardener, dancer, budding internet star, crafter, golfer, or gamer—you can fill in the blank!

Joy Holiday Family

BEST GRANDPARENT COUPON NO.01

BREAKFAST IN BED

007701

SIGN TO REDEEM

X _____

MONTH | DAY | YEAR

BEST GRANDPARENT COUPON NO.02

NAP
without interruption

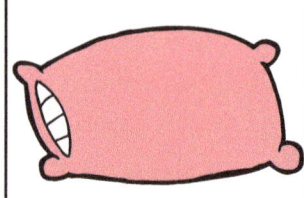

007702

SIGN TO REDEEM

X _____

MONTH | DAY | YEAR

BEST GRANDPARENT COUPON NO.03

SLEEPING IN
undisturbed

007703

SIGN TO REDEEM

X _____

MONTH | DAY | YEAR

HOW DID WE HAVE FUN?

Who

What

Where

BEST GRANDPARENT COUPON NO.04

Make MILKSHAKES or FRUIT SMOOTHIES together

007704
SIGN TO REDEEM
X
MONTH DAY YEAR

BEST GRANDPARENT COUPON NO.05

Go to the PARK

007705
SIGN TO REDEEM
X
MONTH DAY YEAR

BEST GRANDPARENT COUPON NO.06

SLEEPOVER

007706
SIGN TO REDEEM
X
MONTH DAY YEAR

HOW DID WE HAVE FUN?

Who

What

Where

BEST GRANDPARENT COUPON NO.07

FINGER PAINTING

007707
SIGN TO REDEEM X _____
MONTH / DAY / YEAR

BEST GRANDPARENT COUPON NO.08

listen to & laugh at
1 JOKE

007708
SIGN TO REDEEM X _____
MONTH / DAY / YEAR

BEST GRANDPARENT COUPON NO.09

attentively listen to 1 session of
ADVICE

007709
SIGN TO REDEEM X _____
MONTH / DAY / YEAR

HOW DID WE HAVE FUN?

Who

What

Where

BEST GRANDPARENT COUPON NO.10

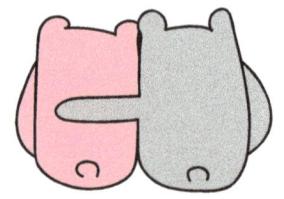

give you one gigantic
BEAR HUG

007710
SIGN TO REDEEM
X _____
MONTH | DAY | YEAR

BEST GRANDPARENT COUPON NO.11

DANCE PARTY

007711
SIGN TO REDEEM
X _____
MONTH | DAY | YEAR

BEST GRANDPARENT COUPON NO.12

house & car
DJ FOR THE DAY

007712
SIGN TO REDEEM
X _____
MONTH | DAY | YEAR

HOW DID WE HAVE FUN?

Who

What

Where

BEST GRANDPARENT COUPON NO.13

LOOK AT FAMILY PHOTOS
together

007713
SIGN TO REDEEM
MONTH DAY YEAR

BEST GRANDPARENT COUPON NO.14

WATCH FAMILY VIDEO
together

007714
SIGN TO REDEEM
MONTH DAY YEAR

BEST GRANDPARENT COUPON NO.15

PLANT FLOWERS

007715
SIGN TO REDEEM
MONTH DAY YEAR

HOW DID WE HAVE FUN?

Who

What

Where

BEST GRANDPARENT COUPON NO.16

SCRAPBOOK
together

007716

SIGN TO REDEEM
X _____
MONTH DAY YEAR

BEST GRANDPARENT COUPON NO.17

GO FOR A WALK
together

007717

SIGN TO REDEEM
X _____
MONTH DAY YEAR

BEST GRANDPARENT COUPON NO.18

BIRDWATCH
together

007718

SIGN TO REDEEM
X _____
MONTH DAY YEAR

HOW DID WE HAVE FUN?

Who

What

Where

BEST GRANDPARENT COUPON NO.19

Build a
FORT

007719

SIGN TO REDEEM

X _____

MONTH | DAY | YEAR

BEST GRANDPARENT COUPON NO.20

DRAW PICTURES
of each other

007720

SIGN TO REDEEM

X _____

MONTH | DAY | YEAR

BEST GRANDPARENT COUPON NO.21

PLAY
cards

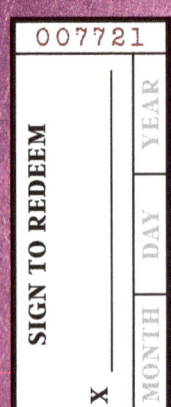

007721

SIGN TO REDEEM

X _____

MONTH | DAY | YEAR

HOW DID WE HAVE FUN?

Who

What

Where

BEST GRANDPARENT COUPON NO.22

LEARN A NEW SONG
together

007722

SIGN TO REDEEM
X _____
MONTH DAY YEAR

BEST GRANDPARENT COUPON NO.23

MOVIE NIGHT
movie of your choice

007723

SIGN TO REDEEM
X _____
MONTH DAY YEAR

BEST GRANDPARENT COUPON NO.24

Play DRESS-UP

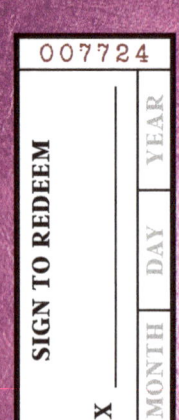

007724

SIGN TO REDEEM
X _____
MONTH DAY YEAR

HOW DID WE HAVE FUN?

Who

What

Where

BEST GRANDPARENT COUPON NO.25

BOARD GAME
of your choice

007725

SIGN TO REDEEM

X _____

MONTH | DAY | YEAR

BEST GRANDPARENT COUPON NO.26

OUTDOOR GAME
of your choice

007726

SIGN TO REDEEM

X _____

MONTH | DAY | YEAR

BEST GRANDPARENT COUPON NO.27

VIDEO GAME
of your choice

007727

SIGN TO REDEEM

X _____

MONTH | DAY | YEAR

HOW DID WE HAVE FUN?

Who

What

Where

BEST GRANDPARENT COUPON NO.28

OUTDOOR ADVENTURE

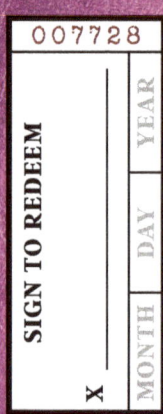

007728

SIGN TO REDEEM

X _____

MONTH | DAY | YEAR

BEST GRANDPARENT COUPON NO.29

BUILD 1 THING TOGETHER

007729

SIGN TO REDEEM

X _____

MONTH | DAY | YEAR

BEST GRANDPARENT COUPON NO.30

FIX 1 THING TOGETHER

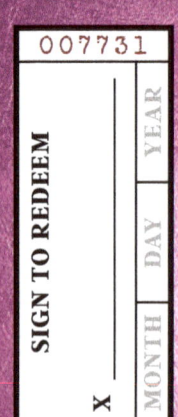

007731

SIGN TO REDEEM

X _____

MONTH | DAY | YEAR

HOW DID WE HAVE FUN?

Who

What

Where

BEST GRANDPARENT COUPON NO.31

WATCH YOUR FAVE SPORT

at home

007731

SIGN TO REDEEM

X _____

MONTH | DAY | YEAR

BEST GRANDPARENT COUPON NO.32

HAVE HIGH TEA

007732

SIGN TO REDEEM

X _____

MONTH | DAY | YEAR

BEST GRANDPARENT COUPON NO.33

PLAY CATCH

007733

SIGN TO REDEEM

X _____

MONTH | DAY | YEAR

HOW DID WE HAVE FUN?

Who

What

Where

BEST GRANDPARENT COUPON NO.34

TAKEOUT DINNER

of your choice

007734

SIGN TO REDEEM

X _____

MONTH | DAY | YEAR

BEST GRANDPARENT COUPON NO.35

HOMEMADE MEAL

of your choice

007735

SIGN TO REDEEM

X _____

MONTH | DAY | YEAR

BEST GRANDPARENT COUPON NO.36

MAKE HOMEMADE PIZZA

of your choice

007736

SIGN TO REDEEM

X _____

MONTH | DAY | YEAR

HOW DID WE HAVE FUN?

Who

What

Where

BEST GRANDPARENT COUPON NO.37

BAKE
FAVORITE COOKIES
together

007737

SIGN TO REDEEM

X _____   MONTH / DAY / YEAR

BEST GRANDPARENT COUPON NO.38

GO SHOPPING
TOGETHER

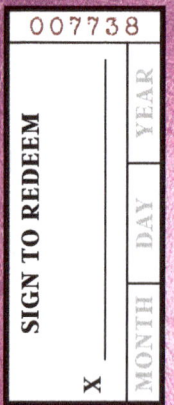

007738

SIGN TO REDEEM

X _____   MONTH / DAY / YEAR

BEST GRANDPARENT COUPON NO.39

COFFEE OF
YOUR CHOICE

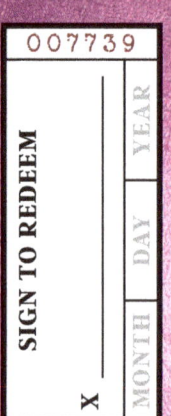

007739

SIGN TO REDEEM

X _____   MONTH / DAY / YEAR

HOW DID WE HAVE FUN?

Who

What

Where

BEST GRANDPARENT COUPON NO.40

RESTAURANT
of your choice

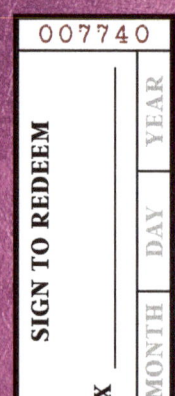

007740

SIGN TO REDEEM
X _____
MONTH DAY YEAR

BEST GRANDPARENT COUPON NO.41

take you out to
ICE CREAM

007741

SIGN TO REDEEM
X _____
MONTH DAY YEAR

BEST GRANDPARENT COUPON NO.42

FOOD TRUCK
of your choice

007742

SIGN TO REDEEM
X _____
MONTH DAY YEAR

HOW DID WE HAVE FUN?

Who

What

Where

BEST GRANDPARENT COUPON NO. 43

DO A PUZZLE
together

007743

SIGN TO REDEEM
X _____
MONTH | DAY | YEAR

BEST GRANDPARENT COUPON NO. 44

Play with
SIDEWALK CHALK

007744

SIGN TO REDEEM
X _____
MONTH | DAY | YEAR

BEST GRANDPARENT COUPON NO. 45

Listen to each other's
STORIES

007745

SIGN TO REDEEM
X _____
MONTH | DAY | YEAR

HOW DID WE HAVE FUN?

Who

What

Where

BEST GRANDPARENT COUPON NO.46

LISTEN TO AN AUDIOBOOK
together

007746

SIGN TO REDEEM

X _____

MONTH | DAY | YEAR

BEST GRANDPARENT COUPON NO.47

Trace each other's
HANDS

007747

SIGN TO REDEEM

X _____

MONTH | DAY | YEAR

BEST GRANDPARENT COUPON NO.48

watch a
COOKING SHOW TOGETHER

007748

SIGN TO REDEEM

X _____

MONTH | DAY | YEAR

HOW DID WE HAVE FUN?

Who

What

Where

BEST GRANDPARENT COUPON NO.49

first pick of the
HALLOWEEN CANDY HAUL

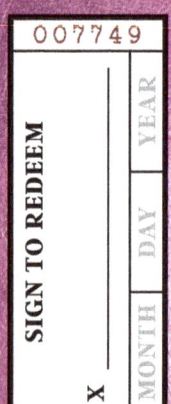

007749
SIGN TO REDEEM
X _____
MONTH | DAY | YEAR

BEST GRANDPARENT COUPON NO.50

BUILD A SNOWMAN
together

007750
SIGN TO REDEEM
X _____
MONTH | DAY | YEAR

BEST GRANDPARENT COUPON NO.51

MAKE POPSICLES
together

007751
SIGN TO REDEEM
X _____
MONTH | DAY | YEAR

HOW DID WE HAVE FUN?

Who

What

Where

BEST GRANDPARENT COUPON NO.52

I will be happy to:
_____
_____

007752

SIGN TO REDEEM

X _____ MONTH | DAY | YEAR

BEST GRANDPARENT COUPON NO.53

I will be happy to:
_____
_____

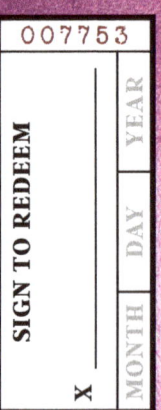

007753

SIGN TO REDEEM

X _____ MONTH | DAY | YEAR

BEST GRANDPARENT COUPON NO.54

I will be happy to:
_____
_____

007754

SIGN TO REDEEM

X _____ MONTH | DAY | YEAR

HOW DID WE HAVE FUN?

Who

What

Where

www.ingramcontent.com/pod-product-compliance
Lightning Source LLC
Chambersburg PA
CBHW040001290426
43673CB00077B/297